This book
belongs to:

....

....

Daddy's Getting Married

Text: *Jennifer Moore-Mallinos*

Illustrations: *Marta Fàbrega*

BARRON'S

When my parents got divorced and Daddy moved
to a different house, it took a little while to get
used to things.

At first I was so mad and upset
that Daddy moved away that I didn't
want to talk to him. When Daddy
would come to pick me up for a visit,
I would cry and scream and make a big fuss.
I guess I thought that if I acted badly, Mom and
Dad would become friends again.

Then one day during my visit with Daddy, he told me that he made a new friend and that he wanted me to meet her. Before I could say NO, Daddy's friend showed up! Not only did I refuse to say HI to her, but I spilled my drink on purpose and didn't even help clean up the mess. Instead I sat with my arms crossed and made a real mean face at her!

Daddy's friend must have really liked him, because no matter how badly I acted and no matter how hard I tried, Daddy's friend wouldn't go away; instead, she was nice to me! Daddy kept telling me that even though he made a new friend, that nothing would ever change and that he would always be there for me, no matter what.

He was right! I talk to Daddy every day on the phone and I visit his house every week. Whenever there's a special occasion, Daddy comes over to my house to help us celebrate. We always have so much fun together that sometimes I forget that Daddy has to leave to go to his house at the end of the night. I always feel a little sad when he goes.

But then things started to change. Whenever I went to Daddy's house for a visit, his friend was always there. I never seemed to have Daddy all to myself anymore! Even though Daddy's friend is pretty (but not as pretty as Mom), and she's really nice to me, especially when she helps me with my math homework, I still miss being a family with just Mom and Dad.

Sometimes when I'm all alone, I dream of Mom and Dad becoming best friends again and I wonder what it would be like if we were together as a family, just like before. Maybe if Daddy didn't find a new friend things would be different. But Daddy did meet a new friend and he's getting married!

When my parents told me that Daddy was getting married, I couldn't believe it! I was shocked! Part of me felt sad that my dreams of becoming a family again were never going to come true. The other part of me was mad at Daddy for not giving me and Mommy another chance. I was confused and I didn't know how or what I was supposed to feel! Both Mom and Dad gave me a big hug and promised that nobody could ever take their place as my parents, no matter what!

It took awhile for me to believe that Daddy was really getting married. When Daddy asked me to be a flower girl in his wedding and asked if I could help with some of the wedding plans, I didn't know what to say. I was worried about Mommy and I didn't want to hurt her feelings by being in Daddy's wedding, but I knew I didn't want to say NO either. What was I going to do?

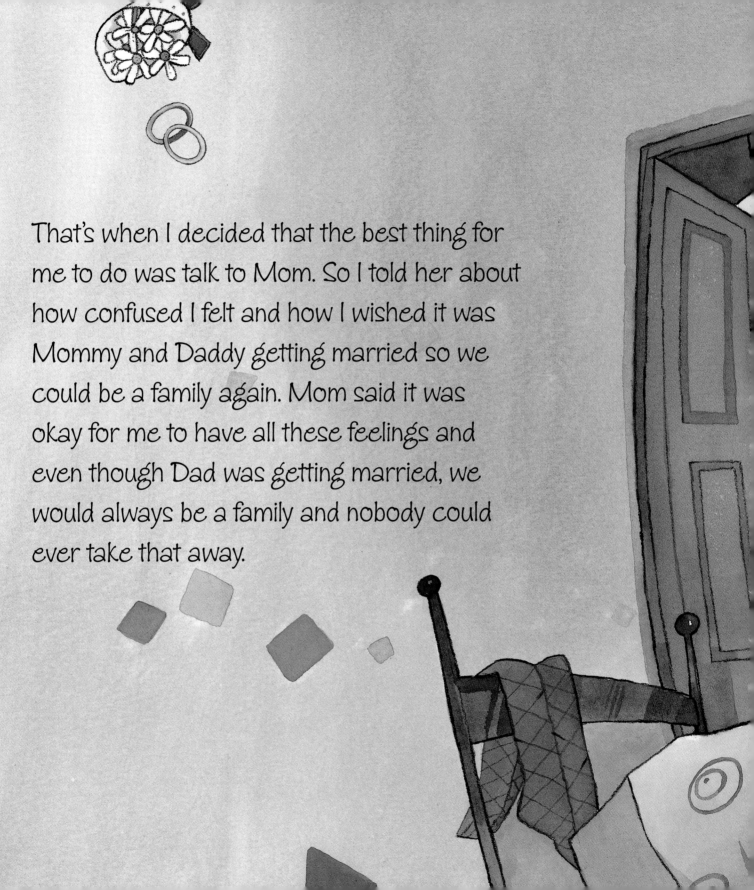

That's when I decided that the best thing for me to do was talk to Mom. So I told her about how confused I felt and how I wished it was Mommy and Daddy getting married so we could be a family again. Mom said it was okay for me to have all these feelings and even though Dad was getting married, we would always be a family and nobody could ever take that away.

Daddy was so happy when I decided to be part of his special day. The only thing I still wasn't sure about was what I was supposed to call Daddy's friend? It didn't feel right calling her Mom because I already had a Mom, and I didn't want to call her Auntie because she's not my Aunt. Instead we all decided that it was okay for me to call Daddy's friend by her first name, Cindy.

Planning the wedding took up most of
Daddy's time and even though I had
fun choosing my dress and my flowers,
I sometimes felt a little left out.

It seemed like all Daddy worried about was the wedding and what Cindy wanted. I couldn't wait for the wedding to be over, because maybe then things would go back to normal.

When the big day finally arrived I was so excited! I felt so special all dressed up with my fancy hairdo and big bouquet of daisies.

I smiled for all the pictures just like I promised I would and when it was my turn to dance with Daddy, he gave me the biggest hug ever then told me he loved me. That's when I knew that everything was going to be okay!

After the wedding, everything seemed to go back to normal. I talk to Daddy as much as I want to on the phone, and I visit his house every week. On special occasions Cindy and Daddy come over to my house to help me and Mom celebrate. Even Mommy and Cindy have become friends. When I'm all alone and I think of the family I have now I feel happy. Mom and Dad will always be my parents and nobody could ever replace them, but it's kinda nice having Cindy around, especially since she's really good at math! And guess what? Mom has a new friend now too!

guidelines
to parents

DADDY'S GETTING MARRIED acknowledges the reality of many families in today's society. It explores some of the anxieties and concerns your children may experience during the transition of change within your family when either parent remarries. By allowing your children the opportunity to explore their thoughts, feelings (both good and bad) and even their fears, they will not only feel validated as important members of your family, but they will be reminded that how they feel matters!

This book can be used as an interactive tool to initiate dialogue and stimulate communication between you and your child. DADDY'S GETTING MARRIED is geared in assisting you and your child in taking an important step toward a new and happy family.

Every child's reaction to his or her parent remarrying is different. Some children may seem angry, upset, and perhaps betrayed, while others may appear unaffected, pleased, and for some children, excited. Children within the same family unit may also have very different reactions, much of which may depend on their age, personality, and current relationship with both parents. Therefore, some children may require more time and patience before they are able to accept the situation fully.

If your child seems to be having a difficult time in coming to terms with the situation and appears "stuck" in his or her ability to move forward in a positive way, you may want to consult with your family physician for advice.

There are many ways to interact with your child, all of which are important. Taking the time to read to your child is not only a great way to share a moment together, but it allows you an opportunity to focus your interaction on a specific topic.

As you read through this book, encourage your children to share their thoughts and feelings and to ask questions. Most importantly, provide them with a comfortable, stress-free environment for this to happen. Your understanding and patience will not go unnoticed!

First edition for the United States and
Canada published in 2006 by
Barron's Educational Series, Inc.
Original title of the book in Spanish:
  Mi papá se casa
© Copyright 2006 by Gemser Publications SL
C/Castell, 38; Teià (08329) Barcelona, Spain (World Rights)
Author: **Jennifer Moore-Mallinos**
Illustrator: **Marta Fàbrega**

All inquiries should be addressed to:
Barron's Educational Series, Inc.
250 Wireless Boulevard
Hauppauge, NY 11788
http://www.barronseduc.com

ISBN-13: 978-0-7641-3503-3
ISBN-10: 0-7641-3503-1
Library of Congress Control Number: 2005938278

Printed in China
9 8 7 6 5 4 3 2 1